ALL JAZZED UP!
INTERMEDIATE PIANO SOLO

CHRISTMAS SONGS

ISBN 978-1-4950-9662-4

7777 W. BLUEMOUND RD. P.O. BOX 13819 MILWAUKEE, WI 53213

Visit Hal Leonard Online at
www.halleonard.com

BLUE CHRISTMAS

Words and Music by BILLY HAYES
and JAY JOHNSON

THE CHRISTMAS SONG
(Chestnuts Roasting on an Open Fire)

Music and Lyric by MEL TORME
and ROBERT WELLS

Slowly, freely

Pedal as needed

Faster, pushing ahead

molto rall.

Fast Bossa

DO YOU HEAR WHAT I HEAR

Words and Music by NOEL REGNAY
and GLORIA SHAYNE

CHRISTMAS TIME IS HERE

from A CHARLIE BROWN CHRISTMAS

Words by LEE MENDELSON
Music by VINCE GUARALDI

FELIZ NAVIDAD

Music and Lyrics by
JOSÉ FELICIANO

Swing feel (same tempo)

HAVE YOURSELF A MERRY LITTLE CHRISTMAS

from MEET ME IN ST. LOUIS

Words and Music by HUGH MARTIN
and RALPH BLANE

Wistfully, feel of 2

I'LL BE HOME FOR CHRISTMAS

Words and Music by KIM GANNON
and WALTER KENT

Medium Latin feel

MERRY CHRISTMAS, DARLING

Words and Music by RICHARD CARPENTER
and FRANK POOLER

SILVER BELLS
from the Paramount Picture THE LEMON DROP KID

Words and Music by JAY LIVINGSTON
and RAY EVANS

SLEIGH RIDE

Music by LEROY ANDERSON

Moderate Funk

To Coda

WHITE CHRISTMAS
from the Motion Picture Irving Berlin's HOLIDAY INN

Words and Music by
IRVING BERLIN

WINTER WONDERLAND

Words by DICK SMITH
Music by FELIX BERNARD

Moderate Bluesy Swing